BELONGS TO

_____

FOREWORD

Welcome to this unique coloring book that intertwines the beauty of mandalas with the heartwarming expressions of Labrador Retrievers. This collection offers you relaxation, creativity, and a deeper understanding of your dog's emotions, fostering a stronger bond between you and your cherished pet.

Venture through captivating mandalas blended with intricately illustrated Labradors, each displaying a distinct emotion. Indulge in this soothing activity, promoting mindfulness and tranquility as you meticulously fill in the designs.

For added excitement, try to guess the emotion portrayed by each dog as you color. At the book's conclusion, you'll find a special section with the answers, enabling you to verify your guesses and gain deeper insight into canine emotions.

We hope this coloring book brings you joy, relaxation, and a newfound admiration for our loyal canine companions. Embark on this captivating journey and le your imagination soar.
Happy coloring!

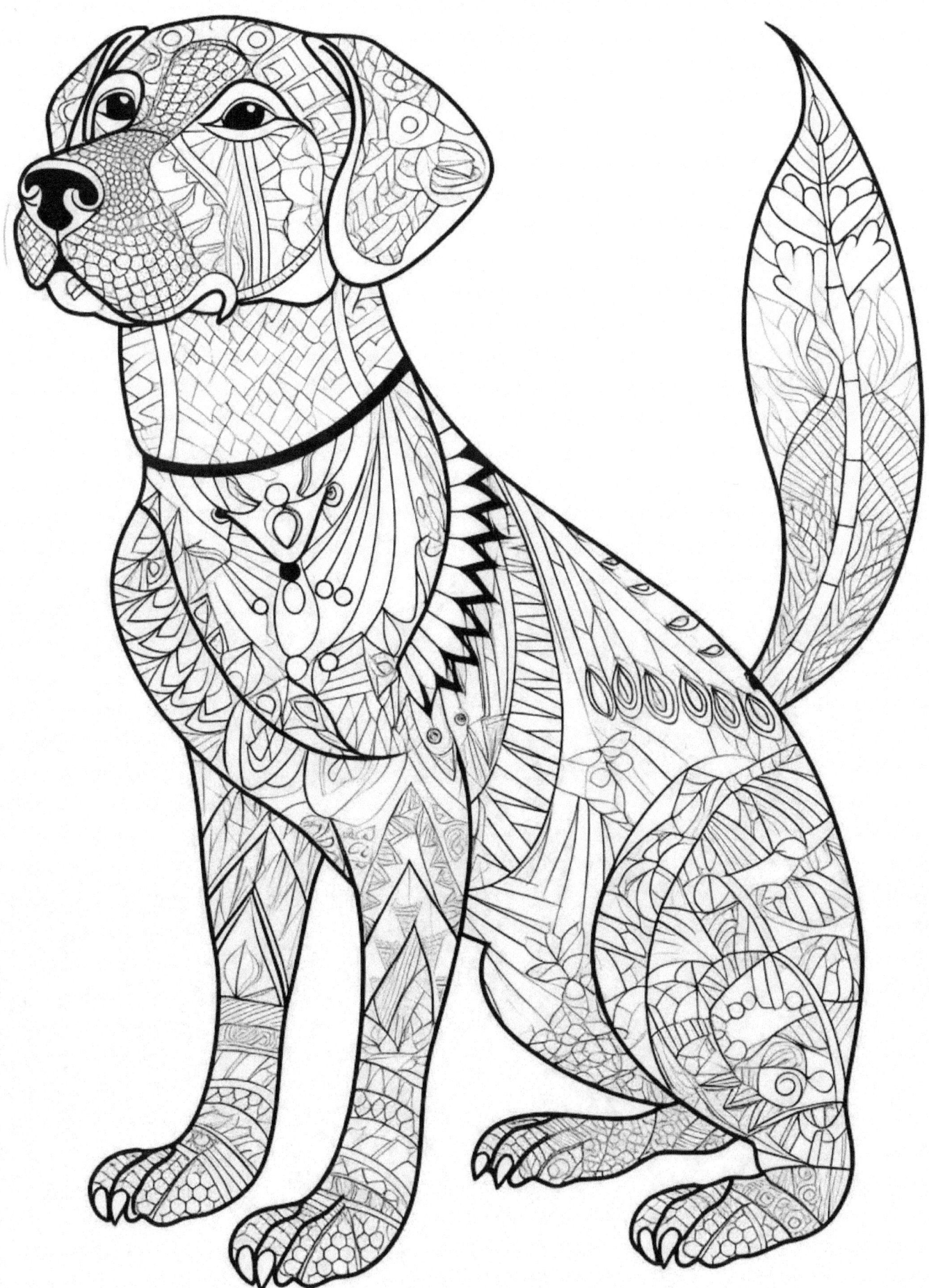

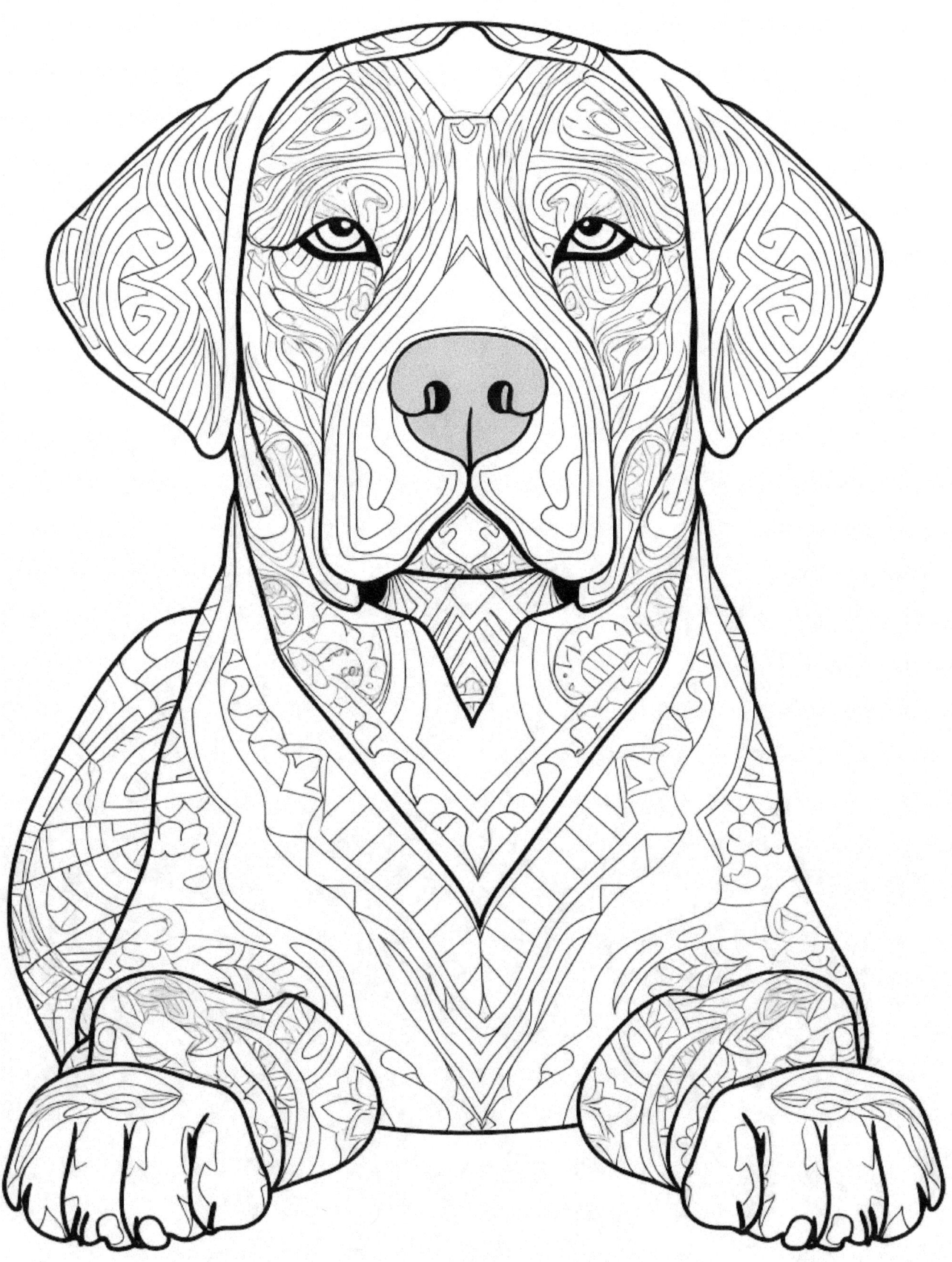

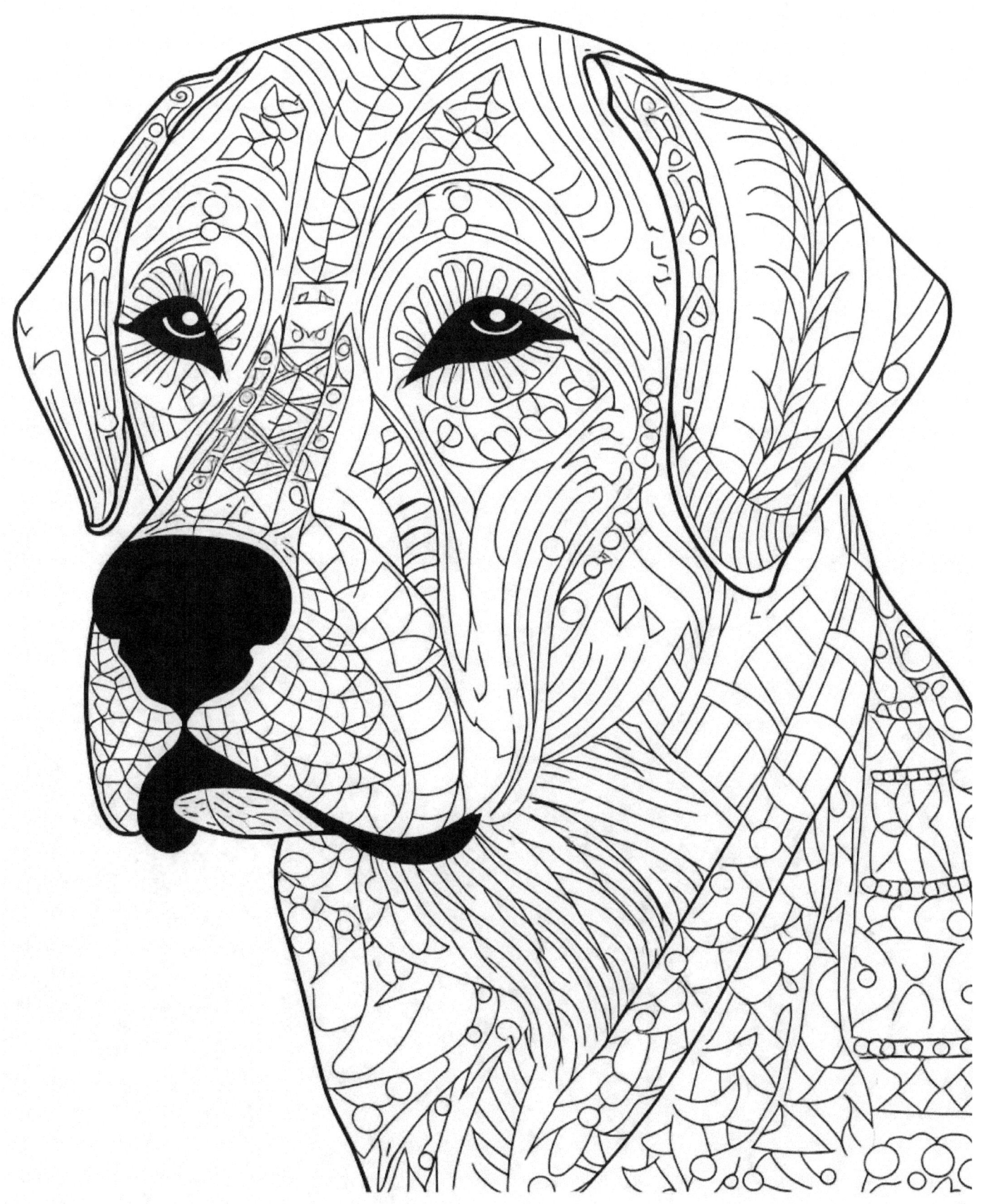

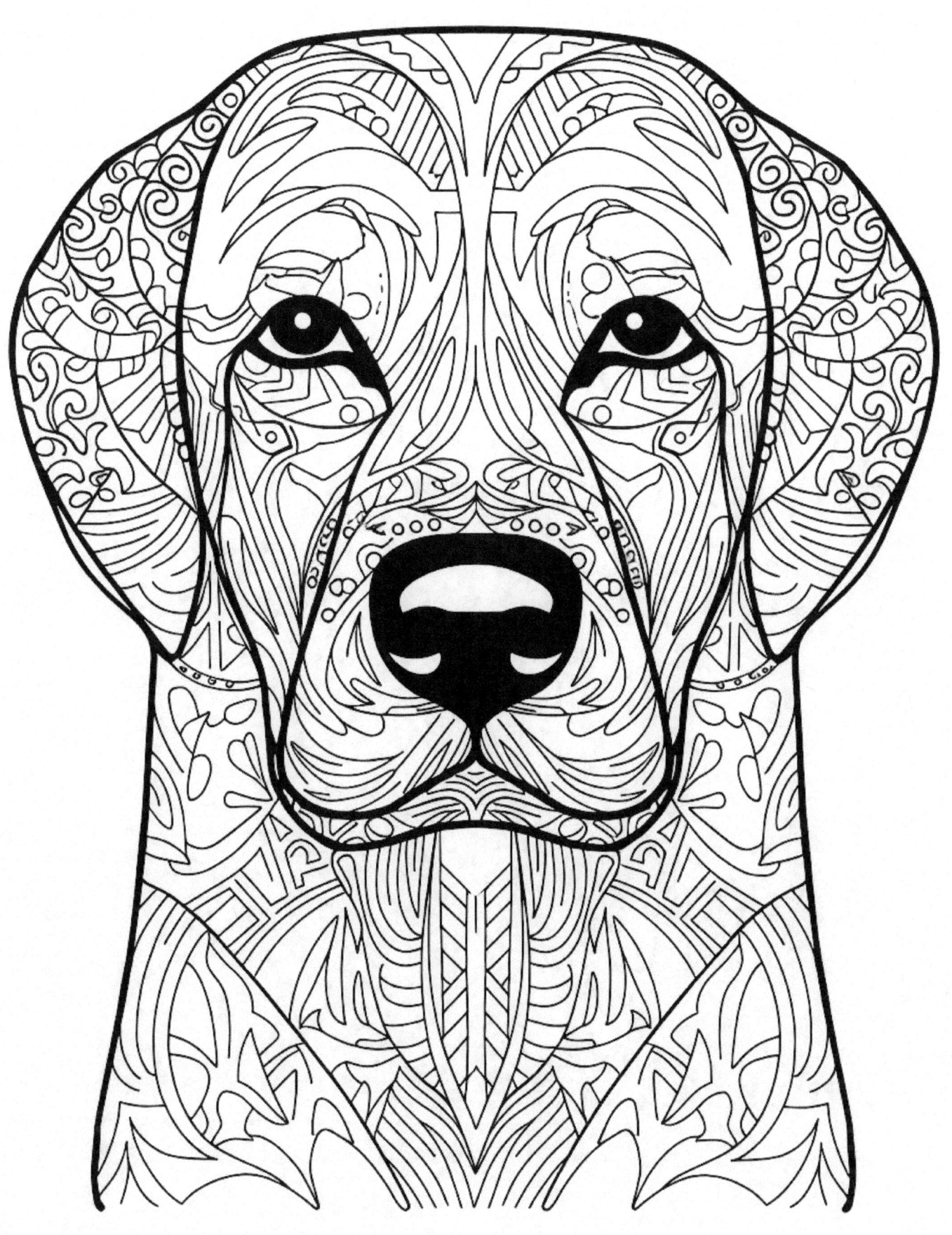

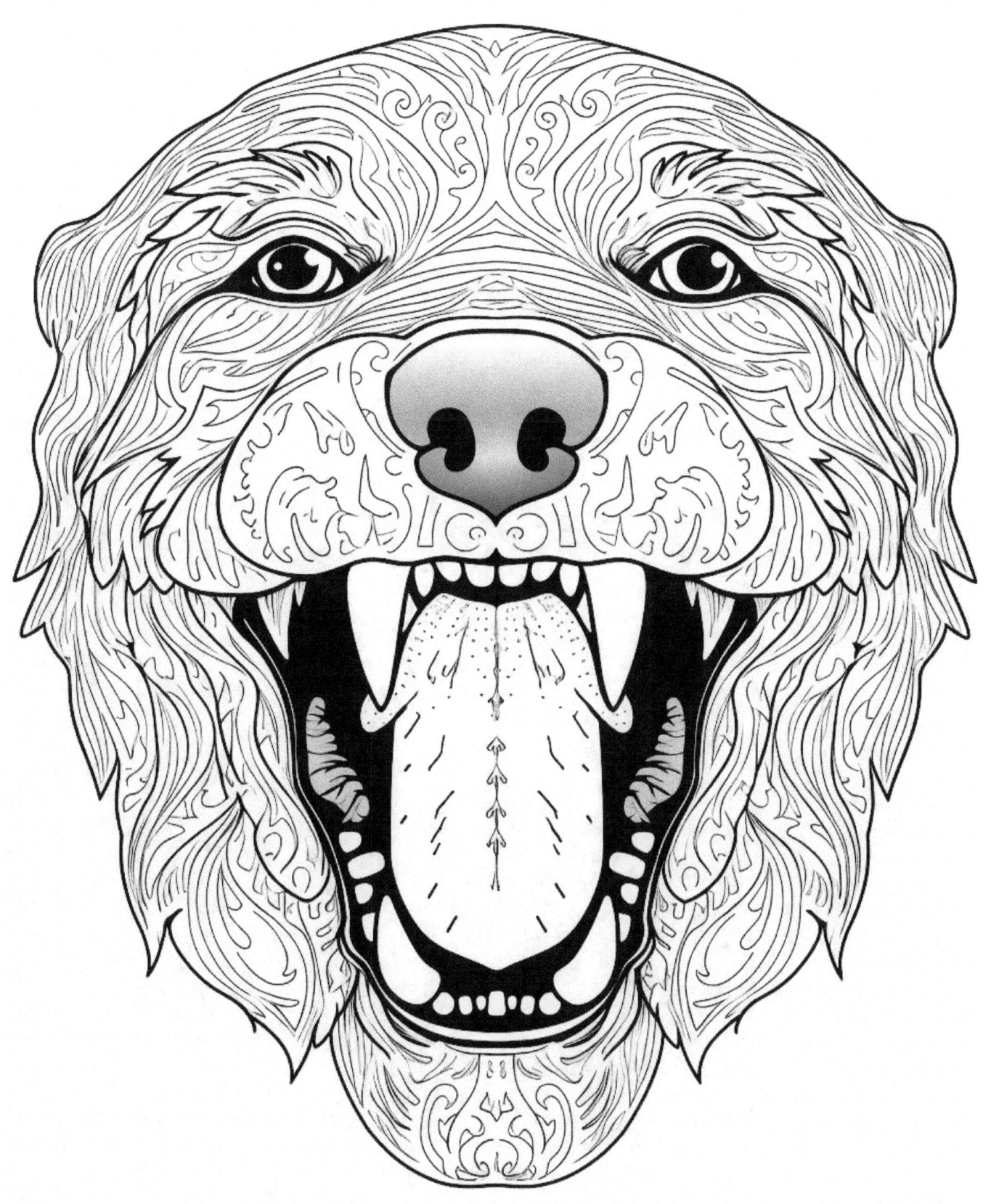

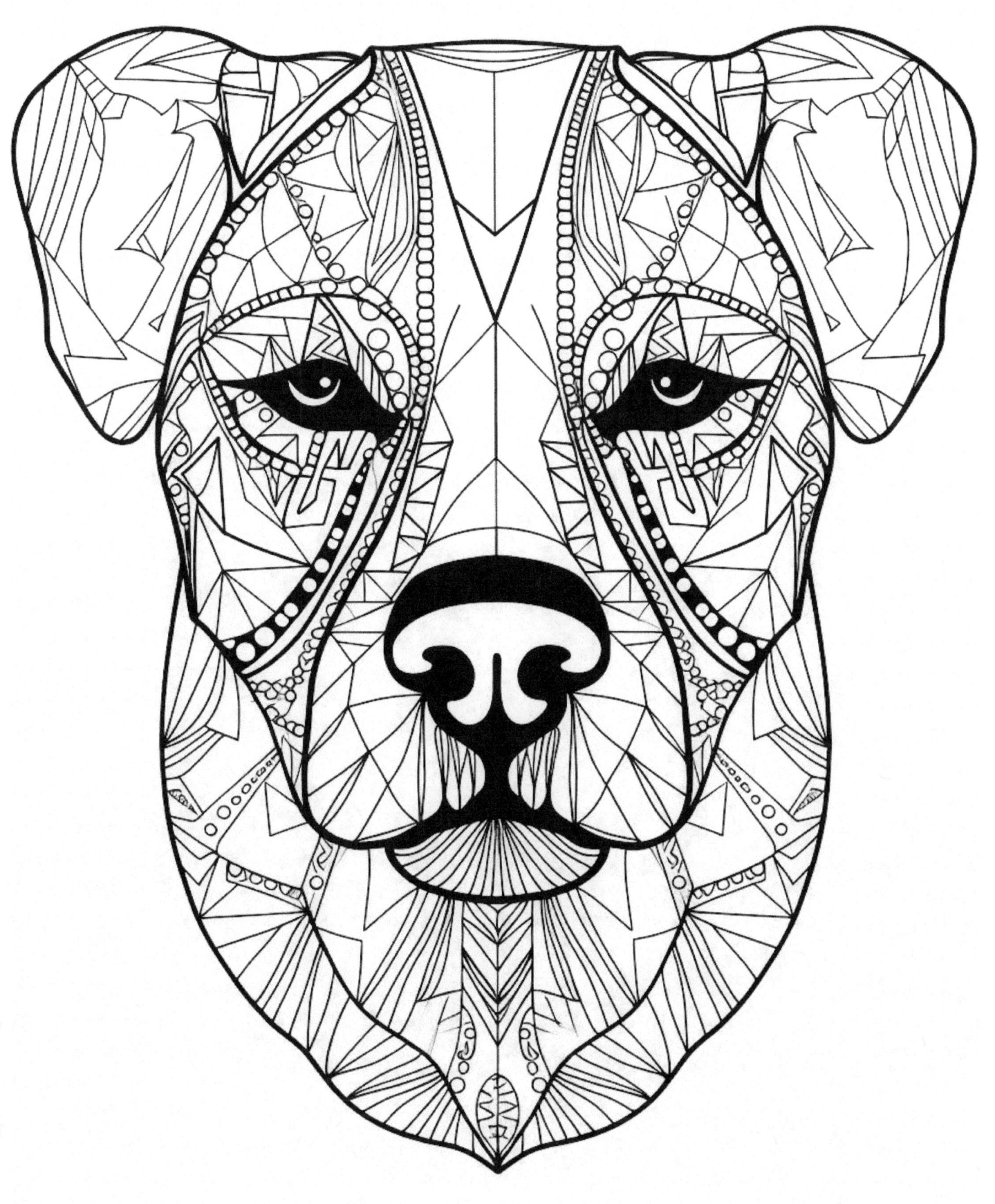

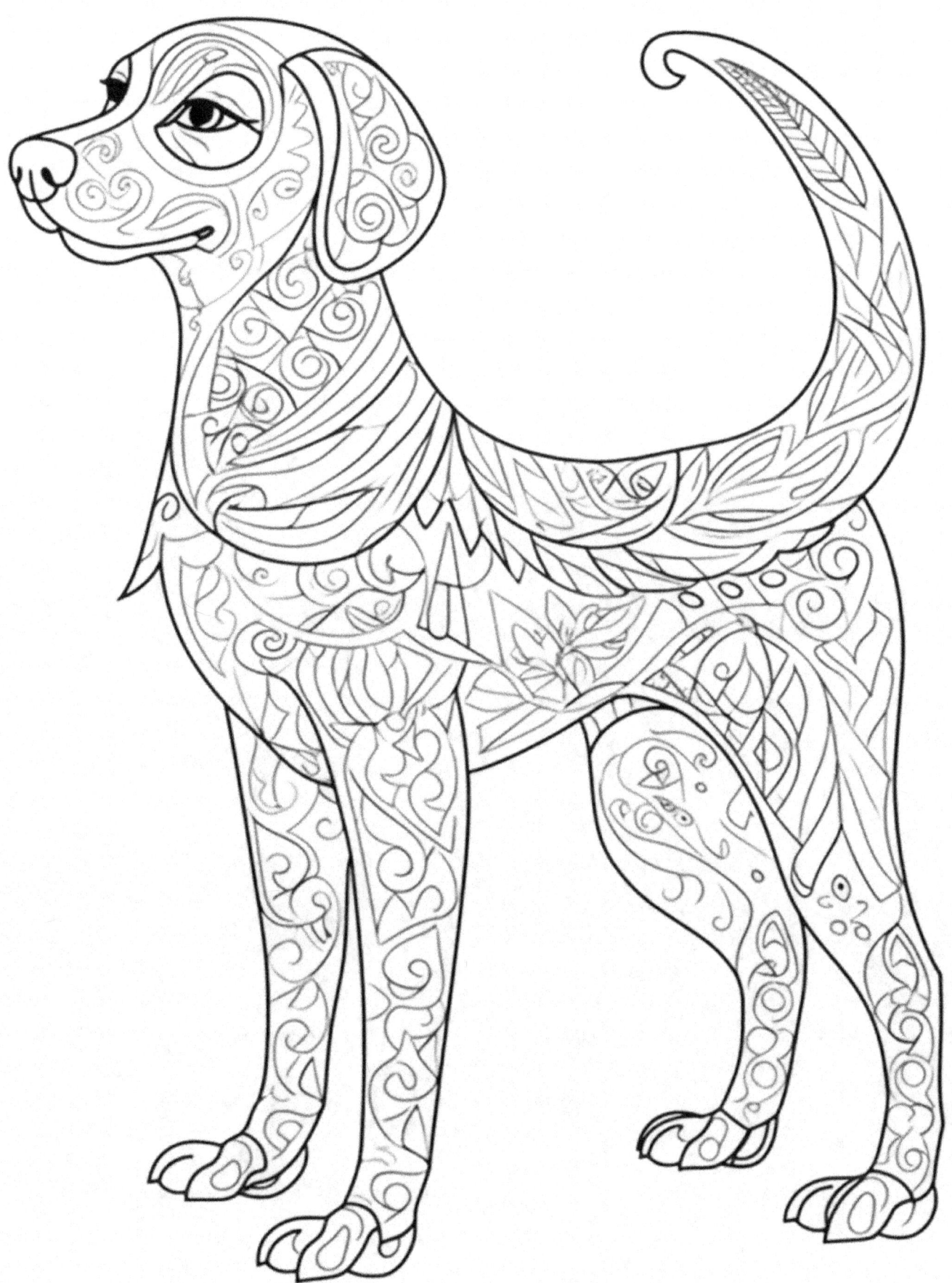

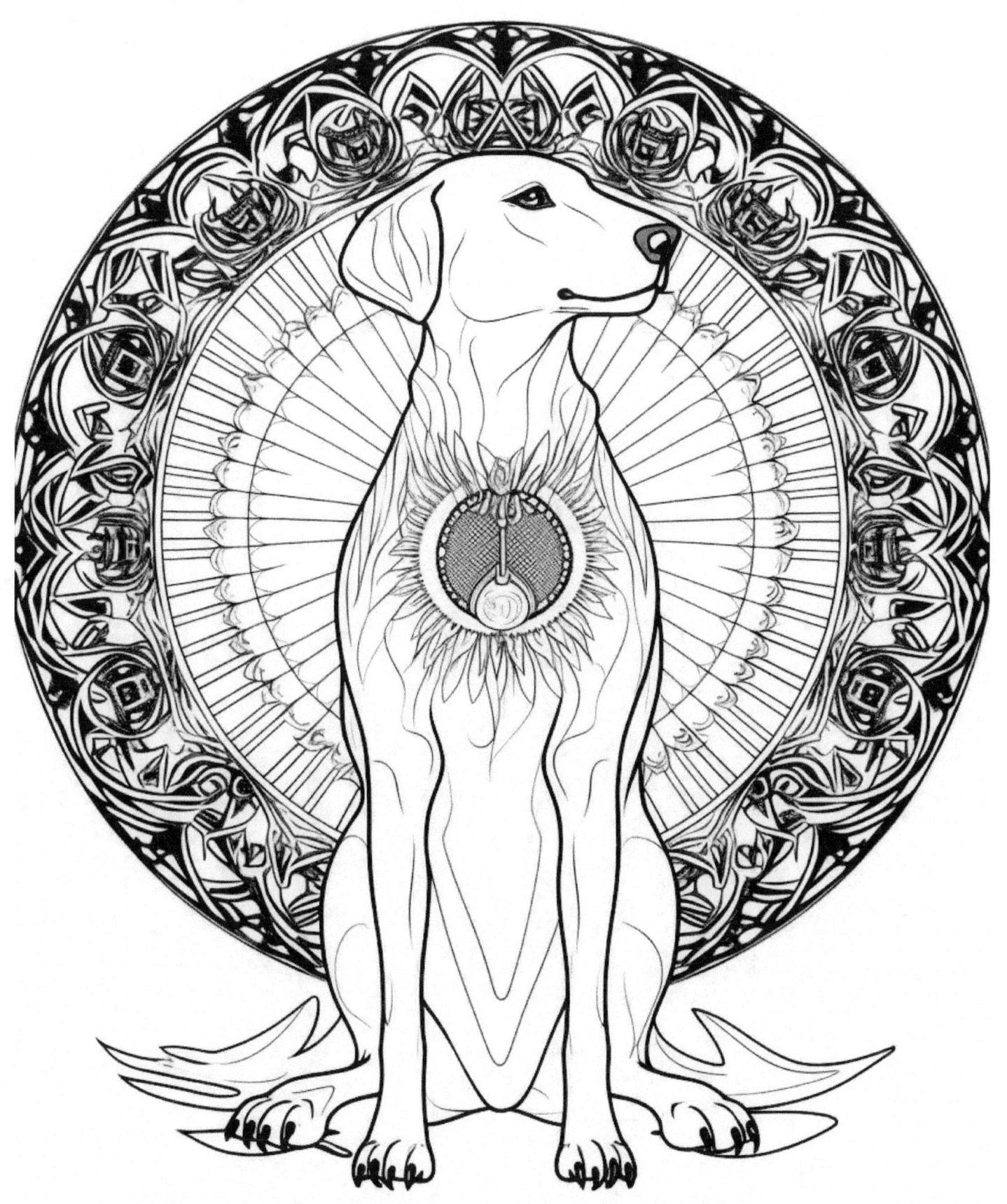

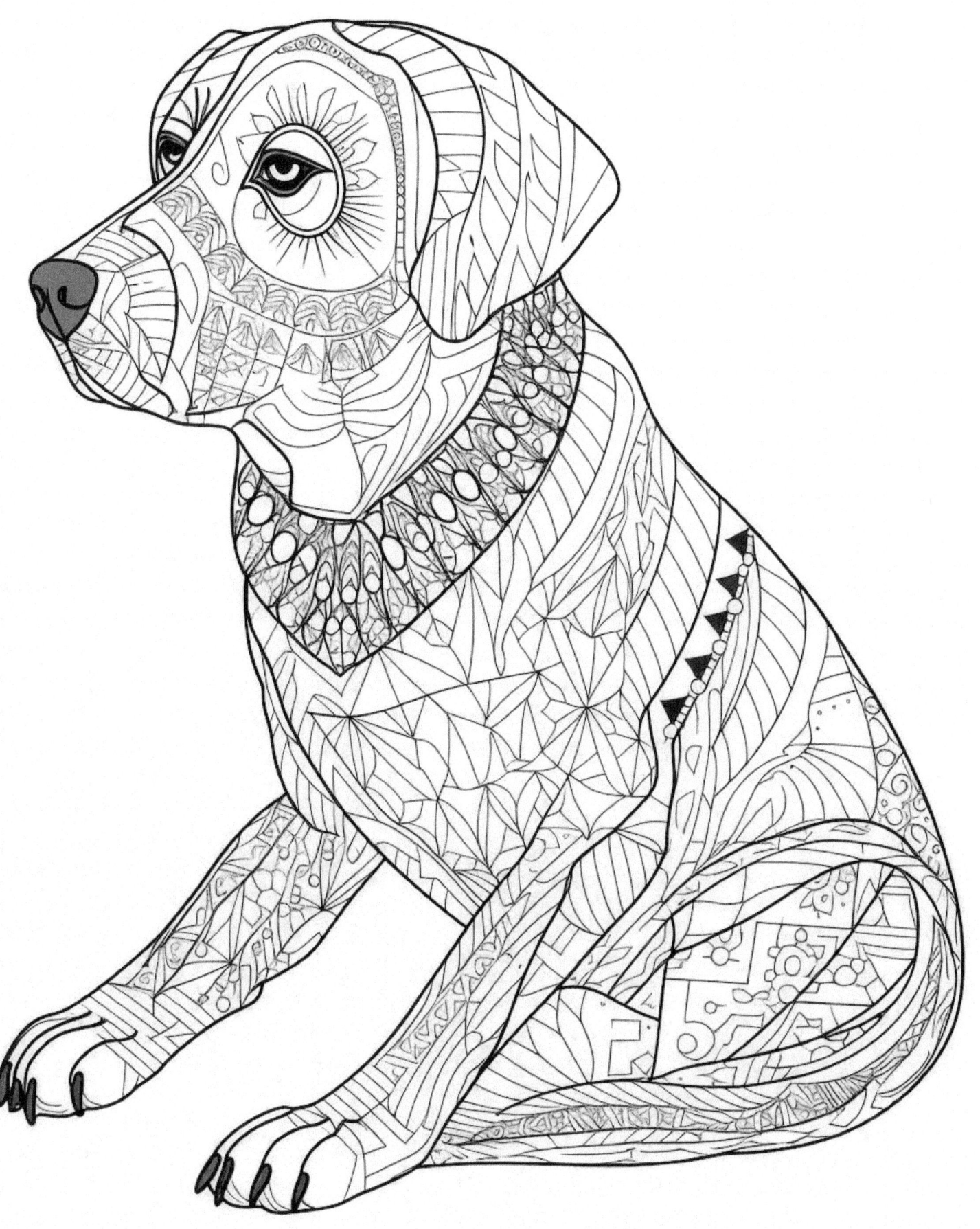

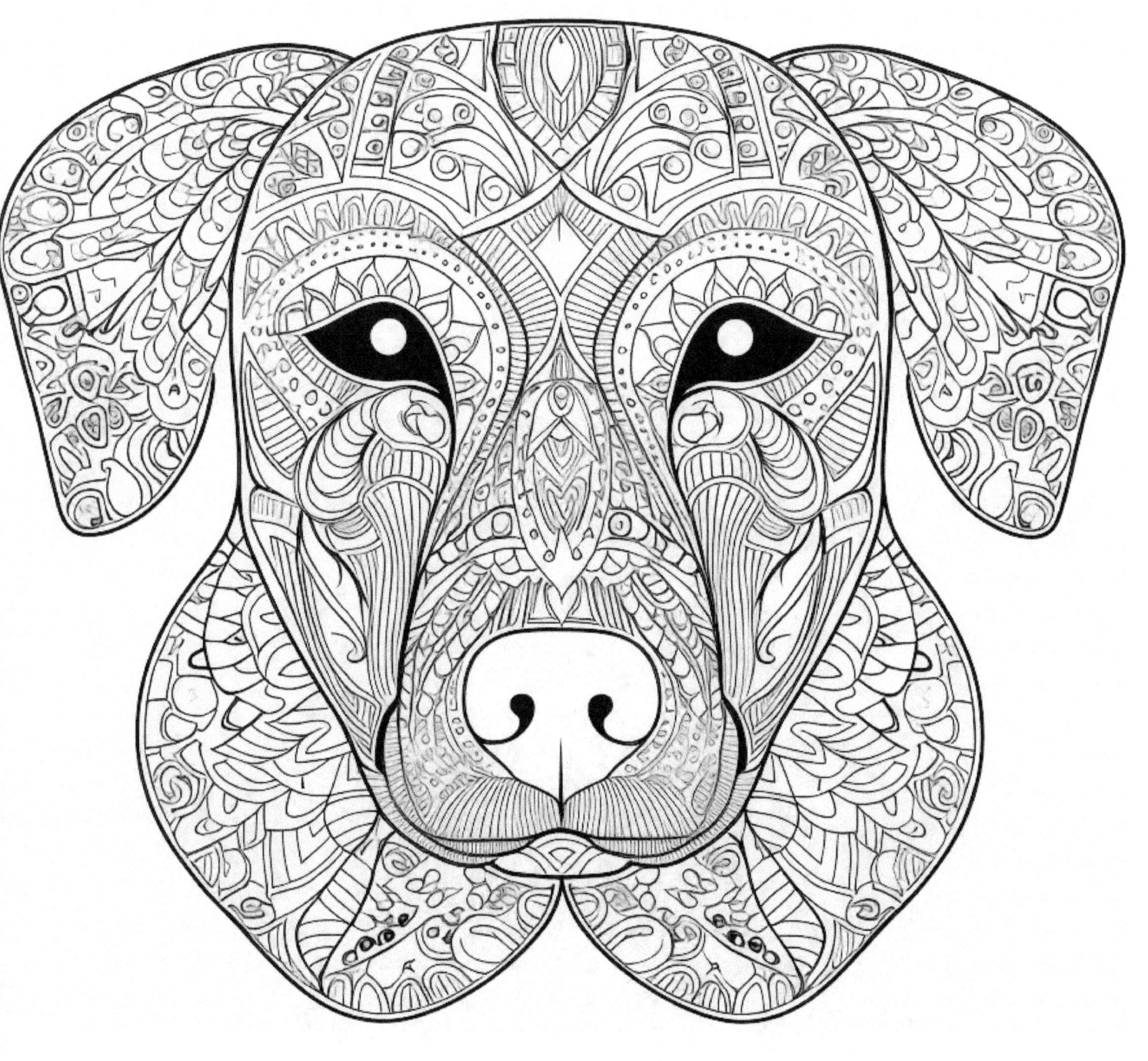

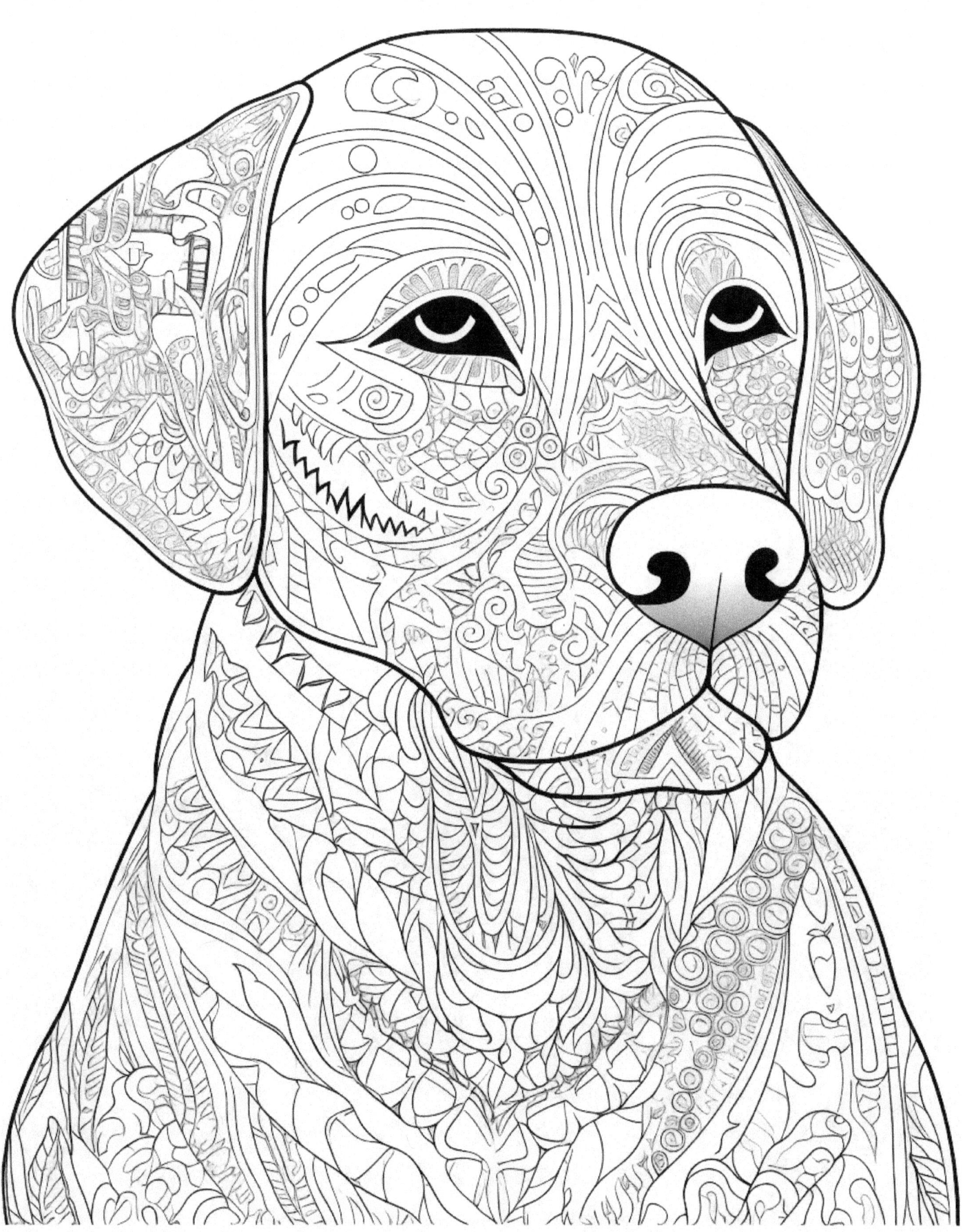

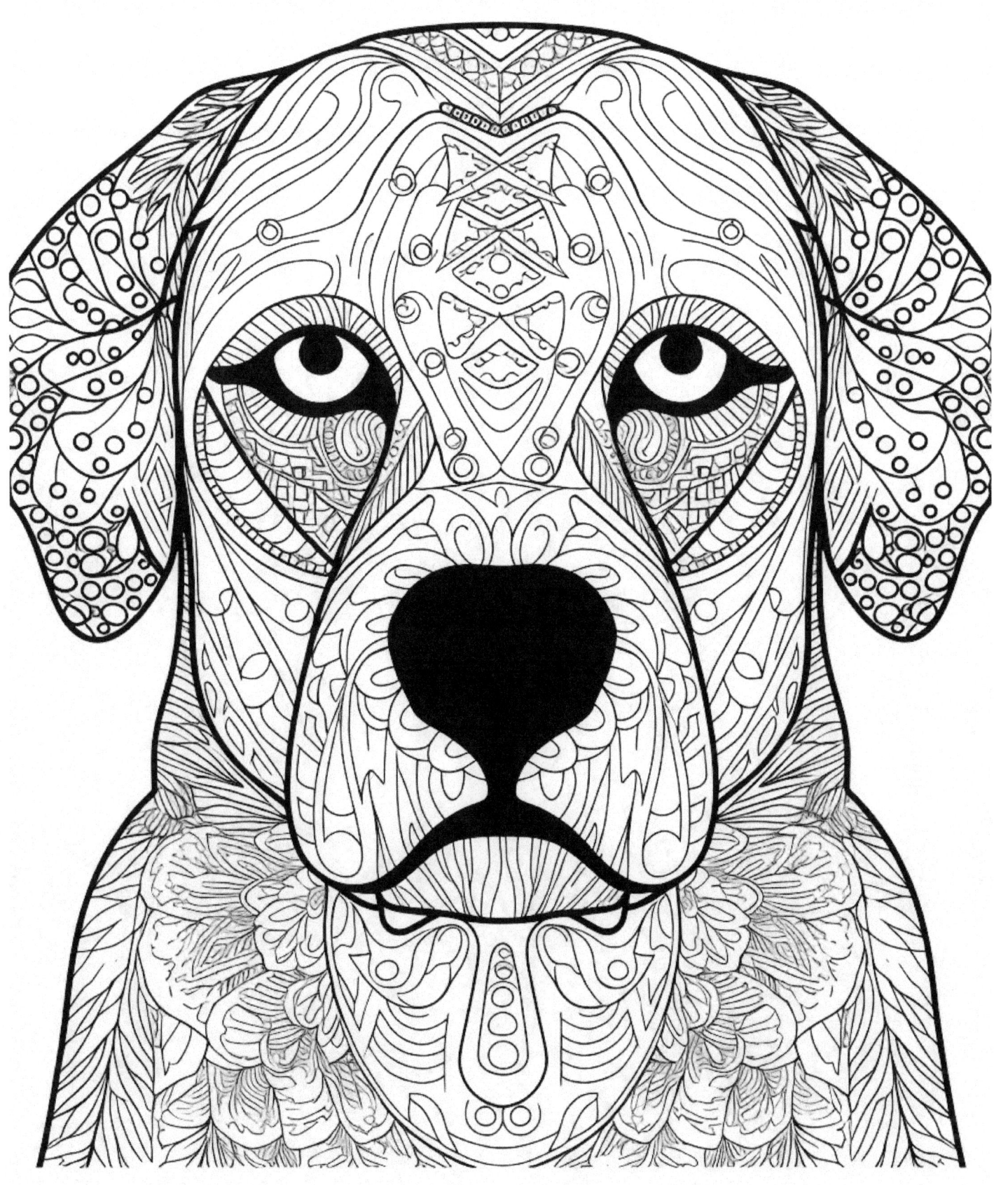

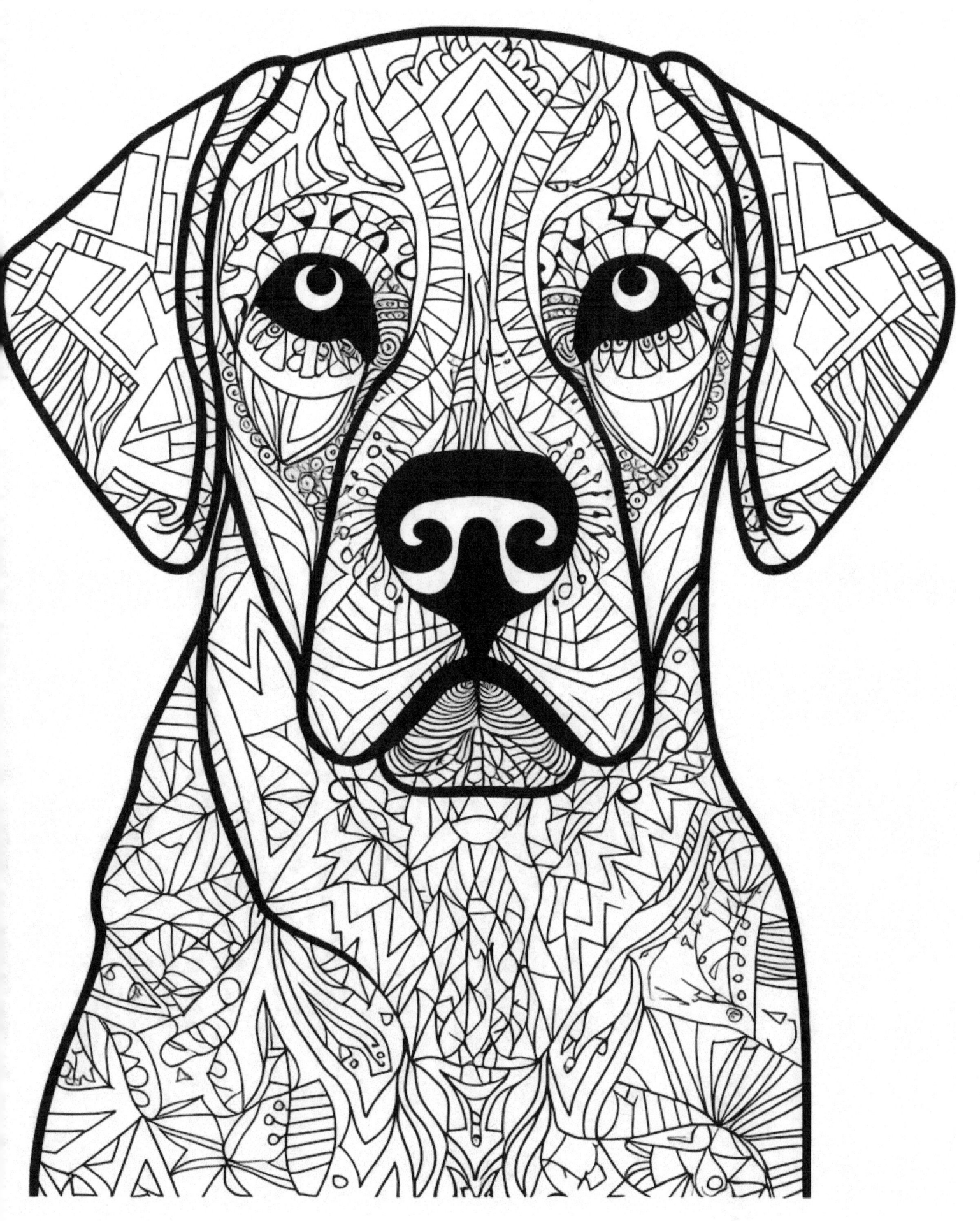

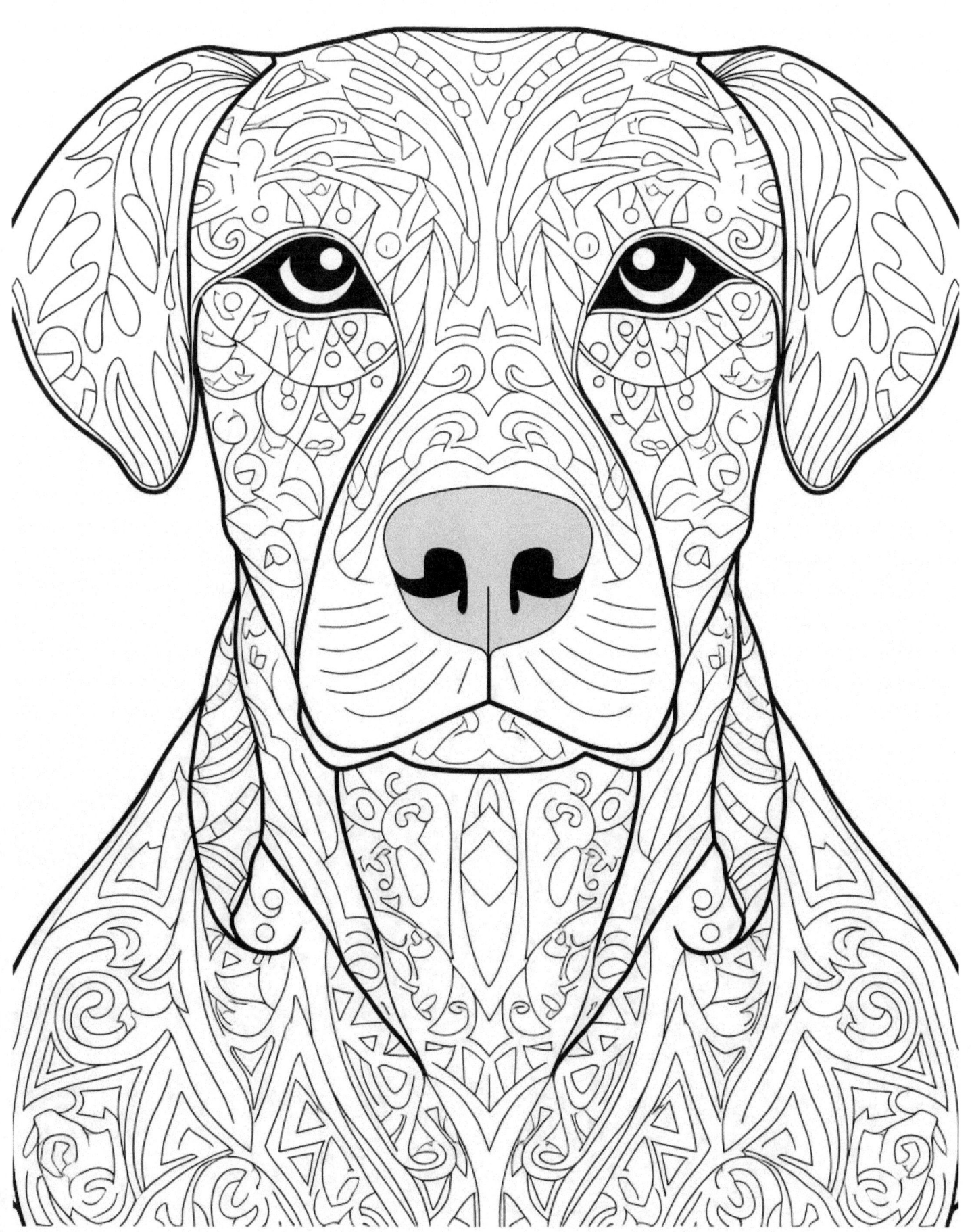

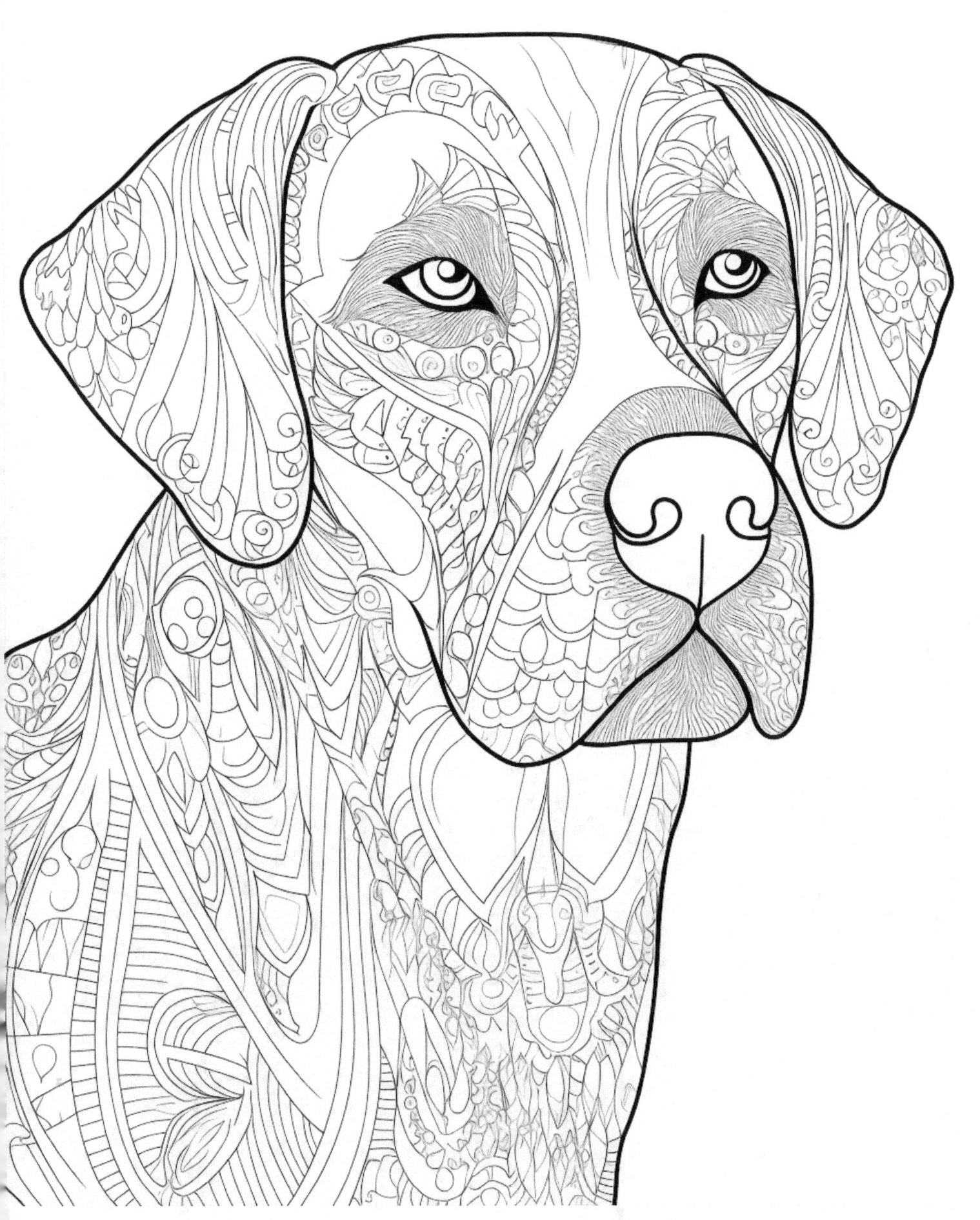

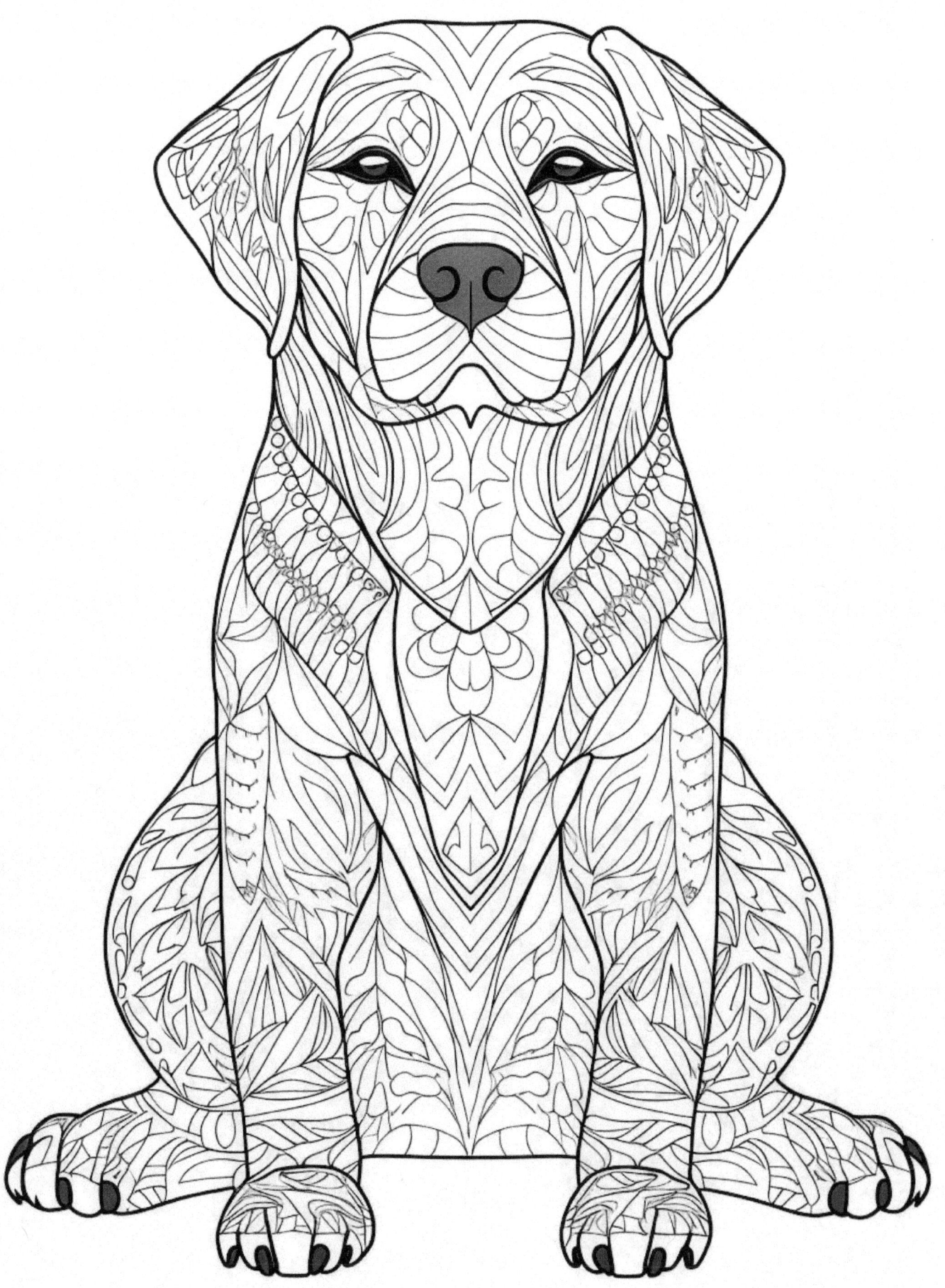

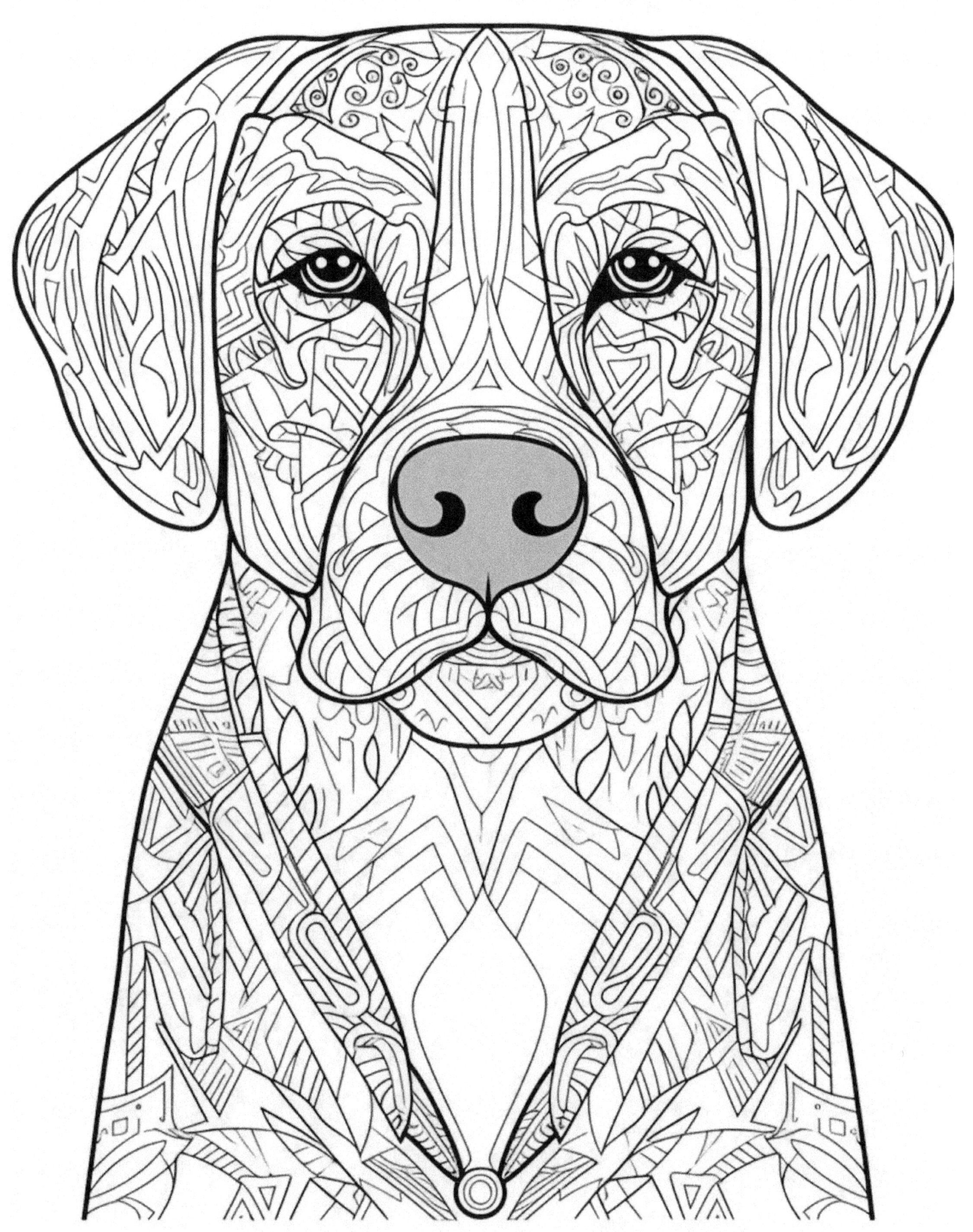

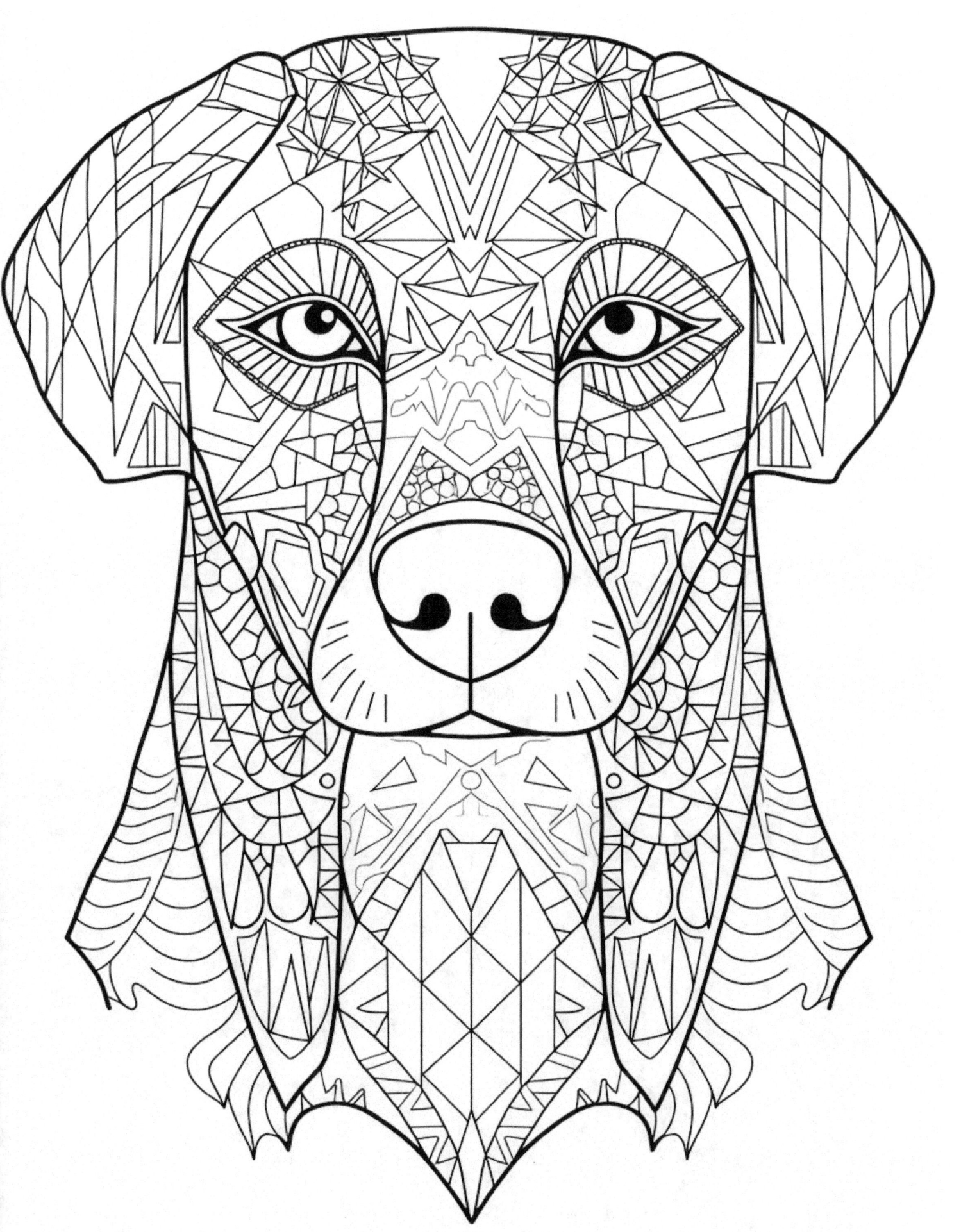

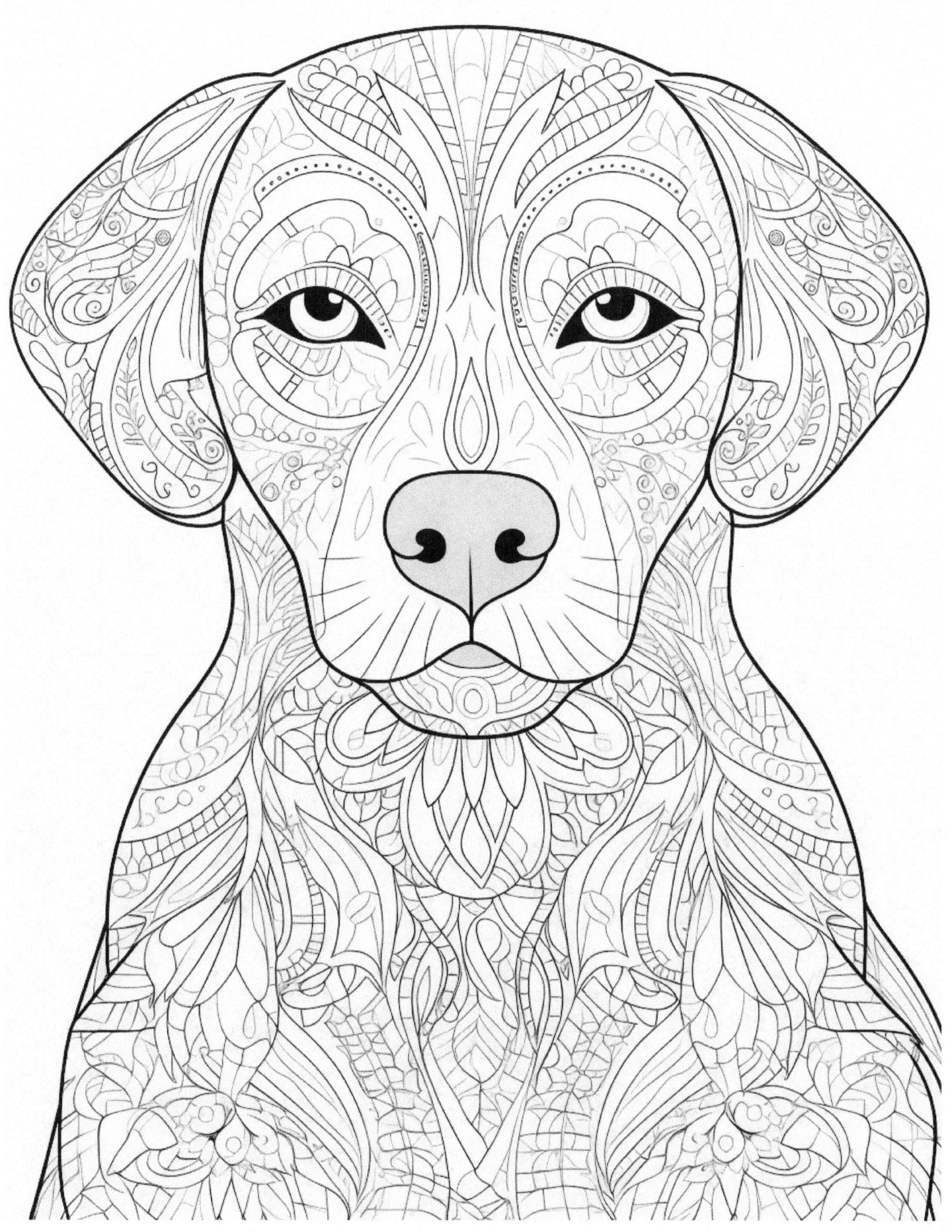

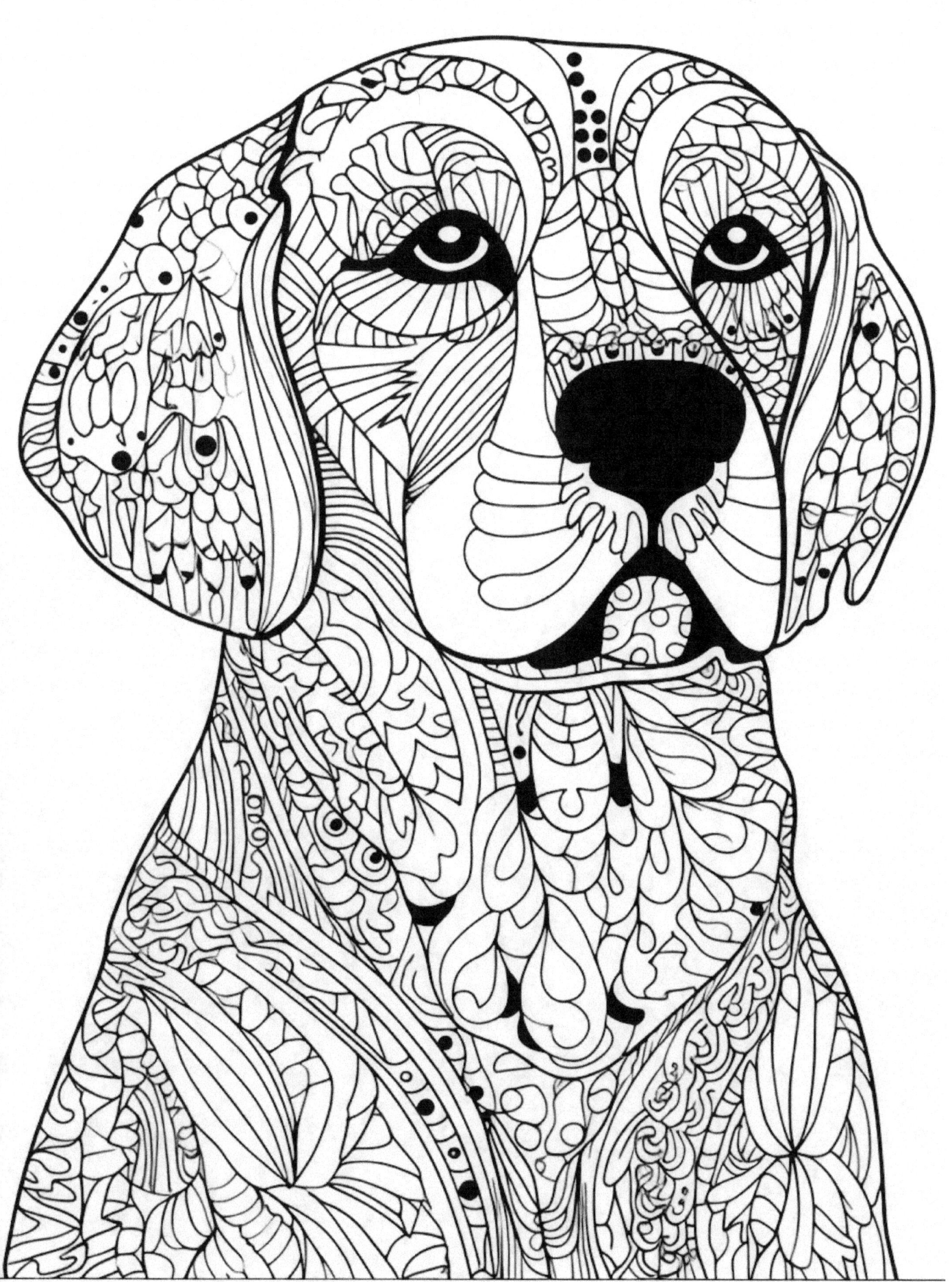

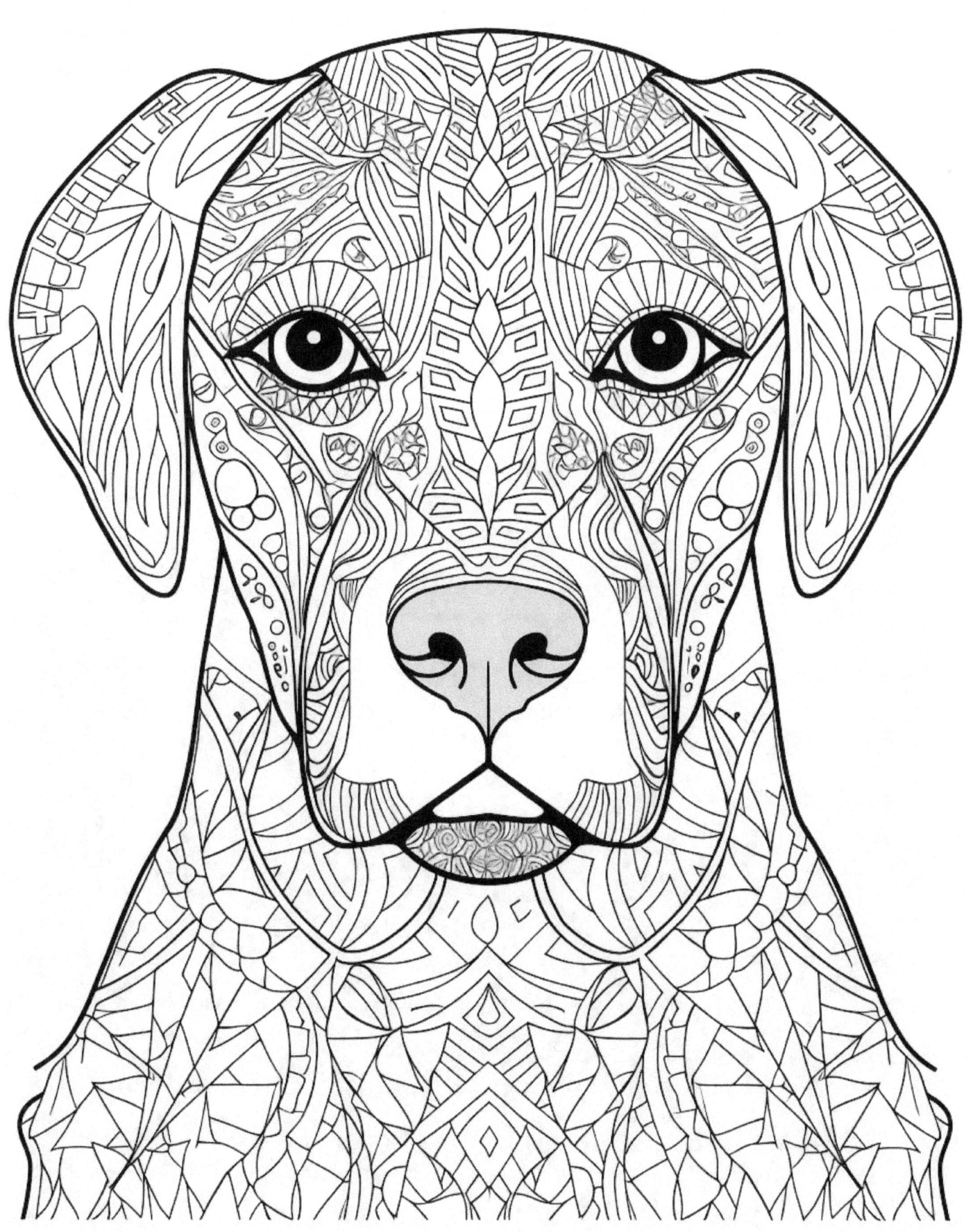

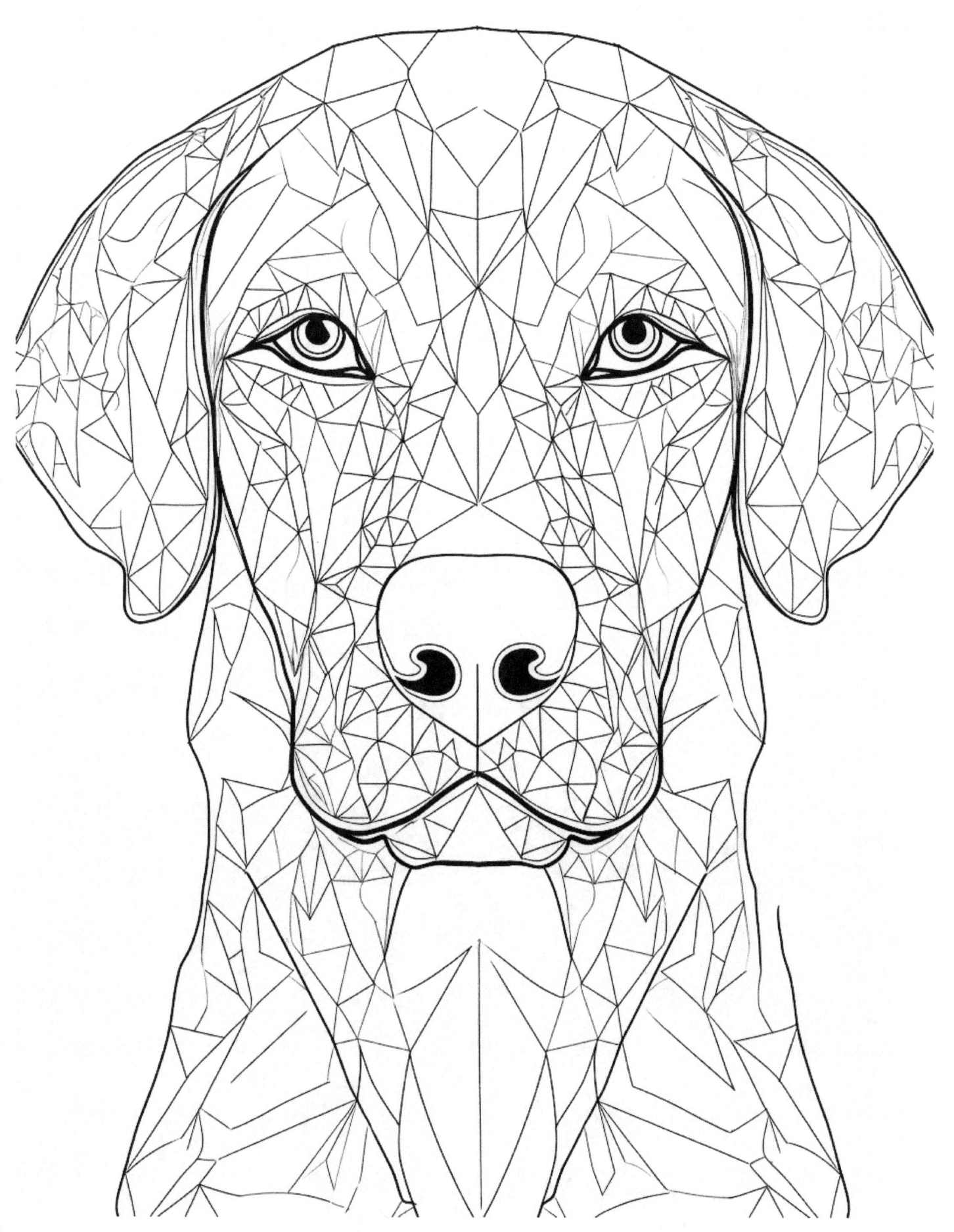

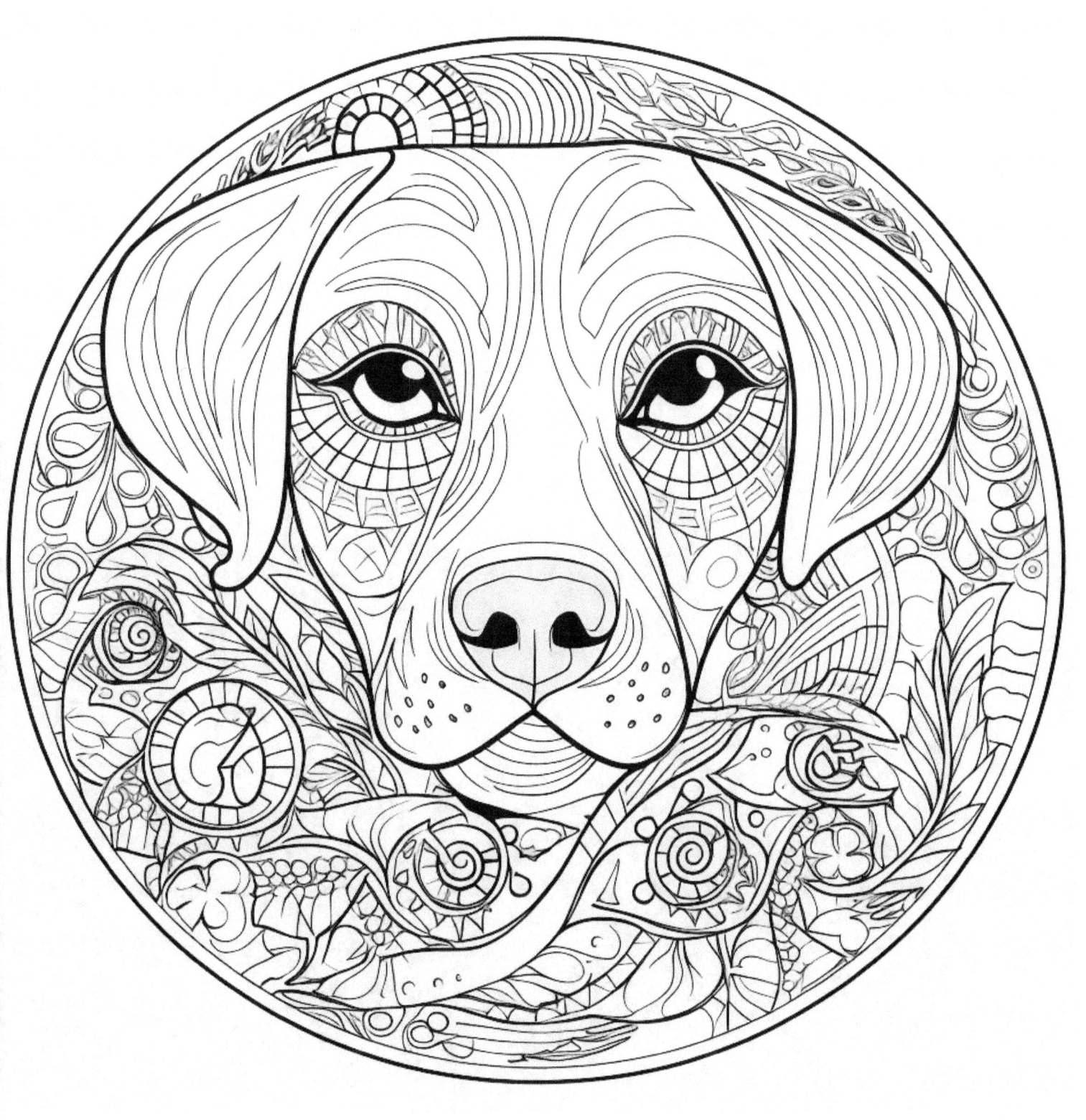

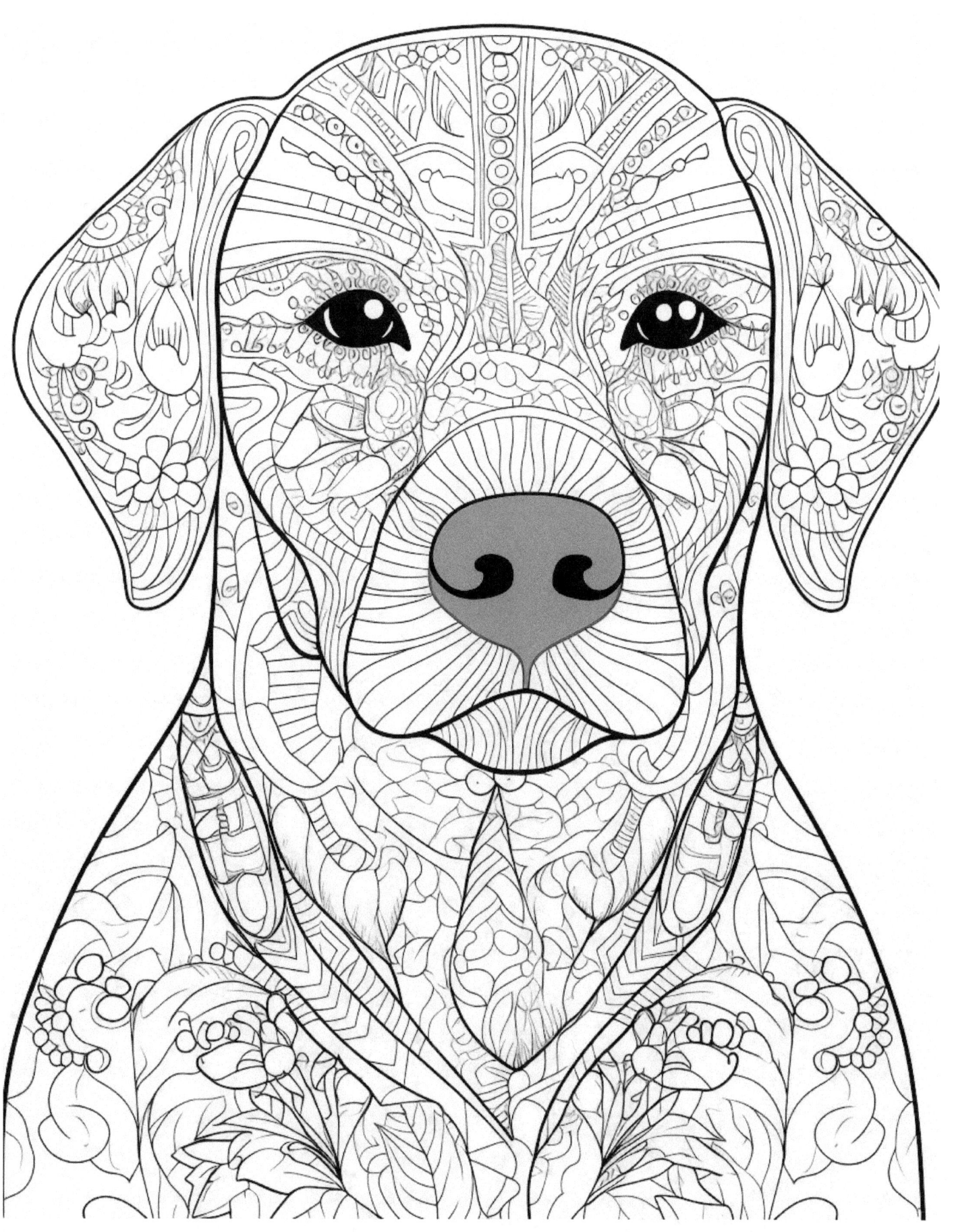

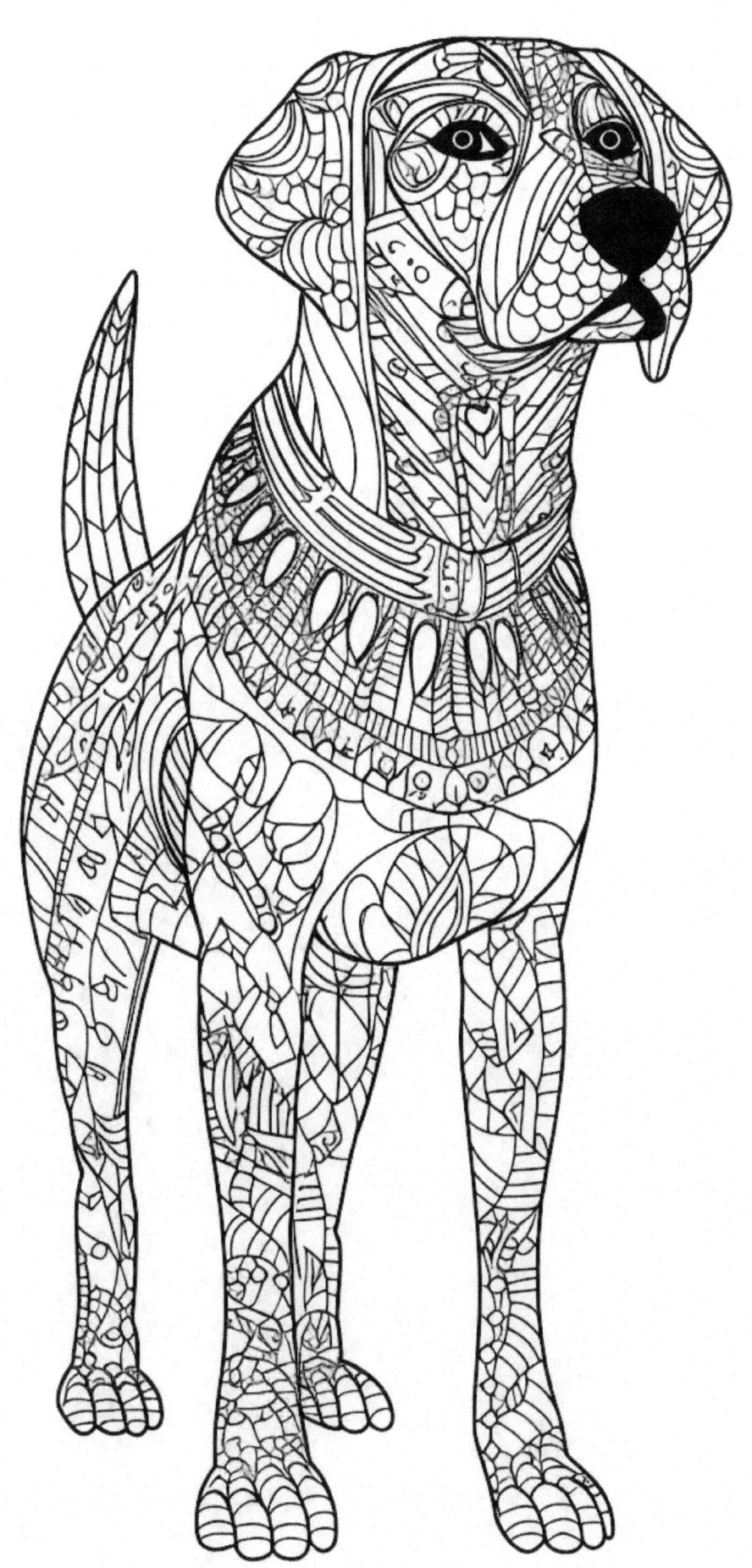

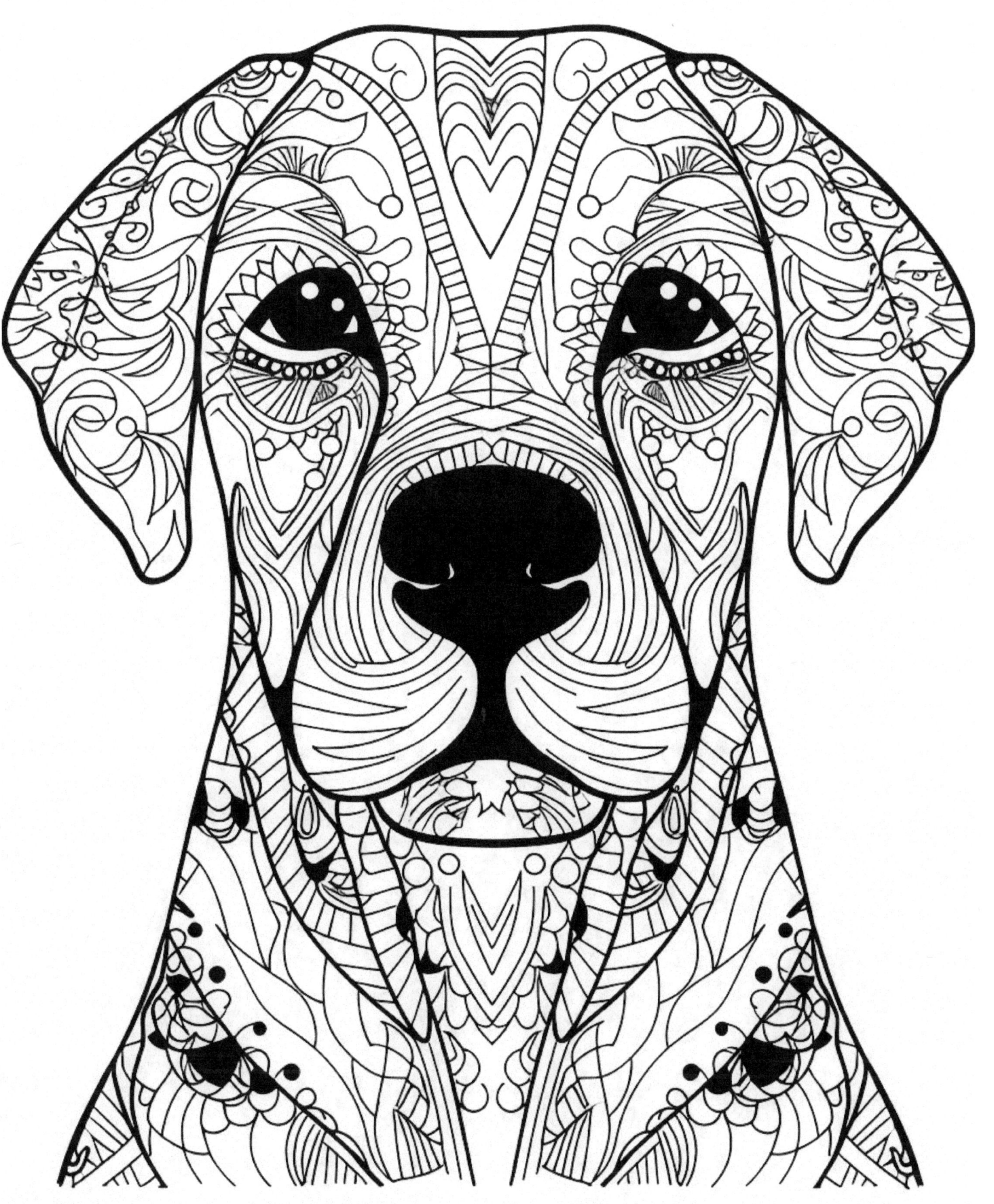

Labrador Expressions: Decoded